# HOW THINGS WORK

# GROOVY
# GADGETS

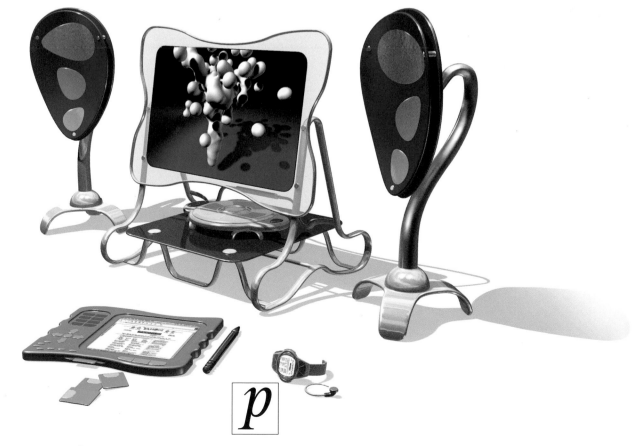

p

This is a Parragon Book
This edition published in 2001

Parragon
Queen Street House
4 Queen Street
Bath BA1 1HE, UK

ISBN 0-75255-294-5

Printed in Dubai, U.A.E

Produced by
Monkey Puzzle Media Ltd
Gissing's Farm
Fressingfield
Suffolk IP21 5SH
UK

Illustrations: Studio Liddell
Designer: Tim Mayer
Cover design: David West Children's Books
Editor: Linda Sonntag
Editorial assistance: Lynda Lines and Jenny Siklós
Indexer: Caroline Hamilton
Project manager: Katie Orchard

Photos supplied by Tony Stone Images 11 (Bruce
Ayres), 24 (Stephen Johnson), 31 (Arthur Tilley),
42 (Jon Riley), and MPM Images.

# CONTENTS

# MOBILE PHONE

**Recall and redial**
Recall brings names, phone numbers, addresses and notes from the memory and displays them on the screen. Redial calls the last number used.

**ON-OFF buttons**
The mobile is switched on and powered up by the ON button. It can receive incoming calls in this condition, but with the display light and other unnecessary circuits switched off to save battery power. When switched off it is unable to send or receive calls, but tiny amounts of electricity still keep the memory active so it remembers its stored information.

**Number (digit) buttons**
These buttons are pressed to call a certain telephone number or to choose numbered options from the lists and menus on the screen.

**Case**
The mobile phone is protected inside a strong plastic case moulded to fit easily in the hand. It may have another cover over the top to cushion the phone from knocks, protect it from splashes and lessen the risk of the phone being switched on or buttons pressed by accident.

**Mouthpiece**
This is a miniature simplified microphone, the same as in a normal telephone handset.

**Hash and star buttons**
The hash (#) and star (*) are used for automated calls when communicating with a recorded voice and computer, where a number button might cause confusion. For example, the hash button may be pressed to show the end of a sequence of digits, such as a credit card number.

**Powerpack**
Rechargeable batteries give many hours of call time and more than a week of standby time (switched on and able to receive calls). They supply only a few volts of electricity. They are recharged by plugging the phone into its power supply recharger which is connected to the mains.

## MORE AND MORE MOBILES

No gadget in history has sold so well and advanced so fast as the mobile phone. In 1998 Finland became the first country to have more mobile phones than fixed phones. By the year 2000 in many countries, more people had mobile phones than those who did not. Some mobiles can be linked to the Internet and have miniature screens on them for truly mobile global communications.

4

## Earpiece
The sounds of the other person's voice come from this miniature, simplified version of a loudspeaker.

## Aerial (antenna)
Radio waves are sent and received by this thin rod. It can be pulled out of the case for better reception, then pushed back in for safety.

RC815

## Display information
The display shows data (information) such as the telephone number you are calling, the number of an incoming call, choices and options like numbers stored in the memory, any messages left on the answer service, the strength of the radio signal and the amount of battery power left. Numbers, letters and symbols on display work by liquid crystal or LCD technology.

## Backlight
The screen is backlit for easier viewing as you press the buttons to make a call. The backlight goes out a few seconds after the last button is pressed to save battery power.

## Option select buttons
Lists and menus can be viewed and changed on the display by pressing these buttons.

## Three-way call
The user can call and speak to one person and then call another person so that all three may talk to each other, in a three-way conference call.

## Special function buttons
The function buttons carry out short-cut tasks such as calling up the list of names and phone numbers stored in the memory or checking on redial or alarm calls.

## HOW MOBILES WORK

A mobile phone is really a low-power radio transmitter and receiver. When switched on it sends out radio signals that are detected by nearby cellular transmitter-receivers. Each of these sends and receives by radio over a local area or 'cell'. Several receivers may send their identity signals back to the phone. The phone then selects the most suitable receiver and establishes connection through it to the network.

The size of a cell varies but is usually a few kilometres across. Cities where more people are packed together have small cells, because each cell can cope with only a limited number of calls. Also tall buildings or hills might disrupt signals and cause dead spots.

If you use a mobile on the move, it detects the fading signal as it moves farther away from the cell's transmitter-receiver. As soon as possible it automatically switches to the stronger signal in the next cell along.

# PERSONAL STEREO

**Audio mini-cassette**
The cassette is a small case of magnetic tape used for sound only (audio). It has two spools. When the tape play direction reverses, the supply spool becomes the take-up spool.

**Playback head**
This detects the varying pattern of magnetic patches on the tape as it slides past and converts them into a similar pattern of electrical signals for the earpieces.

**Tape guide**
Revolving pulleys of smooth plastic guide the tape around corners.

**Play button**
This large button switches on the tape play motor and works a lever that presses the pinch wheel against the motor capstan to make the tape move along.

**Tape reverse switch**
The direction of the tape drive motor and capstan can be reversed so that the tape slides in the opposite direction, when the supply spool becomes the take-up spool. This means you do not have to take out the cassette and turn it over to play the other side.

**Tape select**
Various types of tapes have different particles in the magnetic coating. For better sound quality, these are usually ferric or Fe (iron), $CrO_2$ (chromium dioxide) or metal (a combination of various magnetic metals).

**Fast rewind button**
RW (FR or REW) makes the motor turn the supply tape spool at high speed to wind back the tape.

**Fast forward button**
FF (FWD) makes the motor turn the take-up tape spool at high speed to wind on the tape.

**Pinch wheel**
The rubber pinch wheel pushes or pinches the tape against the motor capstan when the play button is pressed, to make the tape move along.

**Earpiece**
This is an in-the-ear design that fits snugly into the middle part of the ear. The two earpieces are not identical. The plastic cases are shaped differently and marked L and R for left and right ears.

**Motor capstan**
This metal or plastic post is part of the shaft of the electric motor. It whizzes around and makes the tape, pressed against it by the pinch wheel, move along at a constant speed – no matter how much of the tape is on the take-up spool.

**Radio/tape switch**
In the radio position the electricity supply to the tape motors and playback head circuits is switched off.

## CASSETTE TAPE

Mini-cassette audio tape is about 4 millimetres (one-twelfth of an inch) wide and some 260 metres (715 feet) long for a playing time of 90 minutes (C90). It is made of a flexible plastic strip coated with a layer of tiny magnetic particles, and on top of this is another layer for protection and smooth running past the playback head.

# INSIDE THE EAR

Headphones or earpieces work in a similar way to loudspeakers. In the 1970s earpieces became much smaller while still giving clear, loud sounds, especially to low or bass notes. This improvement was due to new and very powerful combinations of magnetic materials, such as samarium-cobalt. There are various earpiece designs:

- In-the-ear as shown here.
- Around-the-ear with a flexible plastic loop that hooks around the back of the ear flap.
- Side-entry where the earpiece is shaped like a button but fits sideways into the ear leaving an air gap around it. This type is worn on a headband.
- Headphones also have a headband over the top of the head. A foam-edged, cup-shaped cushion fits over the whole ear to help cut out sounds from the surroundings.
- Some headphones have fluid-filled cushions that mould themselves exactly to the shape of the person's ear.

**Take-up spool**
This does not pull the tape along. The motor capstan and pinch wheel do that. But it does rotate gently with a built-in ability to slip, to keep the tape taut as it is fed through.

**Battery compartment**
Two small long-life alkaline batteries give enough electrical power to play tapes for up to 10 hours or to listen to the radio for more than 20 hours.

**Radio display**
The numbers on the display show the frequencies of the radio waves, that is, how many waves per second. For example a station broadcasting on 100 MHz (megaHertz) means it produces about 100 million radio waves each second.

**Mini jack plug**
The standard mini jack plug is rod-shaped and 3.5 millimetres (one-twelfth of an inch) wide. It has three metal contact bands along its length. The tip and middle bands send electrical signals to the left and right earpieces for stereo sound. The band at the plug's base is 'common' to receive the signals coming back from both earpieces.

**Tuning control**
Turning this knob moves the pointer or indicator along the radio display dial to select different radio stations, by receiving different frequencies of radio waves.

**AM/FM switch**
There are two radio bands called AM (amplitude modulation) and FM (frequency modulation).

**Volume control**
The volume or loudness of the sounds from the earpieces is controlled by this rotating knob.

# GO-PED

**Handlebars**
The rider holds both handlebars and turns them to steer the Go-Ped just like a bicycle.

**Throttle trigger**
The trigger is linked to the engine throttle by a cable. The throttle supplies more fuel and air to the engine to increase its speed and so make the vehicle go faster, up to 32 kph (20 mph).

**Engine kill**
An easily accessible switch cuts off and stops the engine in case of problems or an emergency.

**Handlebar stem**
A safety spring on the stem allows the handlebars to move down so that they are less likely to harm the rider in case of an accident. The handlebars and stem fold flat along the foot deck for carrying and storage.

**Brake lever**
Pulling on the lever works the front caliper brakes by a long cable, as on a bicycle.

## SPECIAL ENGINE

The two-stroke petrol engine is similar to those used in some power tools, and also in certain off-road or track motorcycles. In some Go-Peds it drives the rear tyre via a roller. In others it is linked by a transmission unit that only makes the rear wheel turn as the engine gains speed and power. This allows the vehicle to stay still with the engine running.

**Frame**
The main frame is made of strong but lightweight metal tubing.

**Front fork**
The fork holds the front wheel and tyre, which turn to one side or the other and steer the vehicle.

**Brake**
Caliper brakes make the brake blocks press against the tyre to slow down the vehicle.

**Wheel and tyre**
The tyre is not air-filled (pneumatic) but solid natural rubber. It cannot suffer punctures, yet it still smoothes out lumps and bumps in the road.

# PPT

Personal powered transport is a very busy area for engineers and inventors. The small vehicles use fewer raw materials and much less fuel than a car, reducing demand for natural resources and cutting pollution.

• The Go-Ped 'motorized skateboard' is small, convenient and lightweight, and can be transported easily when not in use. It carries up to 180 kilograms (almost 400 pounds) so it can be used for shopping. However, it is not suited to wet and slippery surfaces.

• Similar two-wheeled scooter or cycle-type designs driven by electric motors are also being developed. They carry rechargeable powerpacks of batteries that are plugged into the mains electricity overnight.

• The mini-bubble car has three wheels like those on a tricycle and is powered by an engine. The wrap-around clear plastic bubble protects the driver from rain and danger.

## UP AND AWAY

Whenever a new vehicle or craft is invented, people begin to hold races and competitions and to test each other's skills. Motorcycles soon evolved into special 'dirt bikes' on which riders negotiate mud, hills, water jumps and fallen logs.

**Fuel tank**
The tank holds the usual mixture of petrol and two-stroke oil designed for two-stroke petrol engines.

**Foot deck**
The rider stands and balances on the deck as the vehicle moves along. He or she leans slightly to the side to go around curves, but not so much as on a motorcycle because the Go-Ped's wheels are so much smaller.

**Engine**
The two-stroke petrol engine drives the rear wheel directly. Whenever it is running the rear wheel turns.

**Centre stand**
Levered on to this stand the Go-Ped stays upright and the rear wheel is off the ground, for starting or for staying still with the engine running and the rear wheel turning.

**Pull start**
With the rear wheel off the ground, the start cord is pulled out sharply to turn over the engine and get it working. Once the engine has been warmed up, it can be started again after being stopped by 'scooting' the Go-Ped along.

# SCUBA

**Tank**
Air or a special mixture of breathing gases is pumped into here. It's at a very high pressure, so a large volume becomes extremely squeezed or compressed into a small space.

**Water pressure**
The surrounding water presses on the high-pressure diaphragm to make the valve open when necessary and to keep up the intermediate pressure in the first stage regulator chamber and the air hose.

**On-Off valve**
This tap seals or closes the tank so air cannot come out into the first stage regulator. It's used to turn the tank 'off' when not in use and also when refilling it.

**First stage regulator**
The first regulator reduces the very high pressure of the air in the tank to an in-between or intermediate pressure in the air hose, about 80-150 pounds per square inch.

**Valve**
The valve keeps the high-pressure air in the tank unless the pressure in the air hose drops, then it lets some air from the tank into the first stage regulator chamber and hose.

**Air hose**
The first stage regulator chamber leads to the flexible air hose that carries the air to the second stage regulator.

## OUT OF BREATH

There are many ways of seeing the underwater world, watching fish swim, admiring the incredible variety and colour of life on the coral reef or even hunting for shipwrecks and buried treasure. Most forms of diving require some equipment. But in free diving the diver has no gadgets, equipment or artificial aids at all. With plenty of care, practise and expert help on standby, some divers can stay under for more than 20 minutes or descend below 150 metres. But such feats are extremely specialized and very dangerous. Most people struggle to stay under for more than a minute or descend to below about 4–5 metres.

# WHAT IS SCUBA?

The letters stand for Self-Contained Underwater Breathing Apparatus. It's a piece of equipment that lets you swim freely underwater for long periods of time, without having to come up for air. Before scuba gear, divers had to hold their breath or they were attached by tubes or hoses which carried air down to them from the surface. They also had to undergo hours of special training and be physically fit and healthy. Scuba gear, after a period of training, can be used by almost anyone. It has opened up the exciting underwater world to millions of people. The early and well-known type of scuba called the aqua lung appeared in the early 1940s. It was developed by Emil Gagnan and the famous French diver, film-maker, writer, conservationist and ocean expert Jacques-Yves Cousteau.

**Depth gauge**
The depth gauge contains a pressure sensor so the divers know how deep they are. Most divers are advised not to go below about 40 metres. The water pressure increases with depth and by this depth it becomes dangerous. When the divers return to the surface the release of pressure on the body may cause the dangerous, even deadly condition called 'the bends'.

**Ambient-pressure diaphragm**
As the diver breathes in the air, pressure in the second stage regulator chamber falls. The outside water pressure pushes on the flexible diaphragm which curves or bows inwards and works a lever to open the valve and let in intermediate air from the air hose.

**Second stage regulator**
This device lowers the intermediate pressure of the air in the air hose, to the ambient pressure in the second stage regulator chamber. The ambient pressure is the pressure of the surroundings where the diver happens to be – that is, the water pressure all around. The regulator self-adjusts so that as the diver goes down and the water pressure on the body increases, the pressure of the breathed-in air also increases. This ensures the pressures are balanced and the diver's chest can expand against the surrounding water pressure, so breathing is comfortable.

**Exhaust**
Breathed out air leaves the mouthpiece by pushing open flap-like valves into the exhaust manifolds, and then out into the water. It produces a stream of bubbles with each breath.

**Mouthpiece**
Air flows from the second stage regulator chamber through the mouthpiece, into the diver's mouth and own breathing system.

**Valve**
The valve opens when worked by the ambient-pressure diaphragm and lever, to let air from the air hose pass into the second stage regulator chamber. This air can then be breathed in.

DEPTH RUN TIME 56 MIN   MAX DEPTH 198 FT   SURFACE TIME 3 HR
0 58 MIN   ALARM CONDITION

# SATELLITE TV

### Dish
The dish is an antenna or aerial that receives radio signals from the satellite broadcast. It must be pointed at exactly the right angle, both sideways and upwards, to receive the strongest signals from the satellite far above. Satellites that broadcast TV programmes are in a special geostationary orbit (GSO) above the Equator of the Earth. So in the northern parts of the world satellite dishes always point south, and in the south, they point north.

### Parabolic mesh
The shape of the dish and its mesh is a parabola or similar curve. This reflects the radio signals and focuses or concentrates them on to the receiver.

## Too Many Dishes
Some people complain that satellite dishes are unsightly. Local laws often prevent them being fixed to historic buildings.

### Receiver arm
The arm holds the receiver unit at precisely the correct distance and angle from the dish to receive the focused signals.

### Offset receiver
Radio signals are detected and turned into electrical signals by the receiver. This is offset, or not in line with the centre of the dish, so it does not get in the way of the incoming radio signals.

## SATELLITE, TERRESTRIAL AND CABLE
Signals for television programmes can arrive at a TV set in one of three main ways.

• Satellite: This is DBS, direct broadcast by satellite. The signals are in the form of invisible radio waves that come from a satellite high in space. They are broadcast over a wide area and the individual dishes of users pick them up. As domestic dishes are quite small, the satellite must send out powerful signals. The main area where the signals can be received is called the satellite's 'footprint'.

• Terrestrial: The radio signals are beamed out by antennae on tall towers or high buildings. They can usually be received by an antenna shaped like a long bar with cross-pieces.

• Cable: The signals are sent as coded pulses of laser light flashing along a fibre-optic cable buried underground. This system is often combined with telephone and computer lines which work in the same way.

## Sockets and connectors
The rear of the satellite box or unit has connections for the aerial wire, TV set, telephone line and other equipment. It may also be linked to a computer network.

## Aerial wire
The aerial wire conveys the electrical signals from the receiver into the satellite 'box' or decoder. It is routed to avoid electrical equipment such as fluorescent lights that might interfere with the signals.

## Satellite box
The 'box' is basically a decoder unit. The signals coming in are in encrypted or coded form. You must pay for a smart card so that the unit can decode them for viewing on a TV set.

## Remote control handset
The handset has all the buttons and controls for the decoder unit. It communicates with the decoder unit using an invisible beam, usually a low-power infra-red (weak heat) beam.

## Power unit shield
A metal case around the power unit prevents it from interfering with the delicate circuits in the rest of the decoder unit.

## Controls
Some of the most important controls are duplicated on the unit itself in case the remote control unit is lost or broken.

## TV guide
All the programmes on all the available channels allowed by the smart card are displayed on the screen. This can take time, since some satellite systems have more than 100 channels.

## Card reader
The smart card slots into a card reader that detects the magnetic codes in the card's stripes.

## Decryption
The signals coming in from the satellite broadcast are encrypted, or 'scrambled'. The method of encryption changes regularly. Only if the smart card is suited for the date and channel, will the decryption unit un-scramble or decode the signals so they can be fed into the TV set.

## Interactive TV
Some decoder units are interactive, that is, they can send as well as receive. The user receives information via the satellite broadcast, for example, from a shopping channel. He or she then uses the handset to send information from the unit via a connection to the phone line, to order goods.

## Smart card
The card has various code numbers represented by tiny patches of magnetism in its stripes. These include the dates and channels that have been paid for. They are matched to the broadcast information coming in with the pictures and sound. If the card is out of date or the channel is not on the accepted list, the unit stops its signals.

# CAMCORDER

## Zoom lens system
There are many lenses in groups along this lens system. Zooming means they move in and out to change the field or area of view. Zooming in is like looking through a telescope – it shows a small area greatly enlarged. Zooming out shows a broader view at less magnification, so the scene looks further away.

## Objective
The large lenses at the front are called the objective because they point at the object – the item or scene that is being recorded. They gather light rays from the scene and begin to bend or focus them as they pass through the lens system inside the camera.

## Zoom return
A spring on a sliding rod makes sure that the lens system slides smoothly for zooming in and out.

## Zoom gearing
This moves the main lens system forwards and backwards to zoom the image in and out.

## Microphone
Two small microphones angled to each side behind the protective grill detect stereo sound, which is recorded on the tape.

## Screen backlight
This switches on the backlight for the screen so that it can be viewed in dull conditions. It can be switched off in bright conditions to save power, when the LCD screen works by reflected light.

## Focus
The focus knob moves the lenses in relation to each other to make the picture clear and sharp.

## Video tape
The electronic signals from the CCD circuits (representing the picture) and microphones (the sound) are recorded on a video tape in the same way as for a VCR. In some designs the cassette is removed. In others the camcorder is plugged into a VCR later to transfer the recording.

## CCD
The charge coupled device (CCD) is like a miniature screen that senses light rays and turns their positions and brightnesses into patterns of digital electronic signals.

## Powerpack
A pack of rechargeable batteries provides power for the motors of the tape recorder and lens movements and for the electronic circuits and display screen.

## Eyepiece
The user looks through this to see the viewfinder, which shows the pictures that the camcorder is taking.

## Viewfinder
Unlike the photographic camera, light rays don't come all the way through the camcorder, so the user cannot see the scene. Instead, a miniature TV screen in the viewfinder shows the user what is being filmed.

## CAMERA-RECORDER
A camcorder is a combination of a video camera and video recorder. The video camera is designed to take many still pictures or images (usually 25) each second. When they are played back they give the impression of continuous movement as on a TV screen. There is no photographic film in a camcorder as there is in a movie camera. The patterns of light rays that form the images are converted into corresponding patterns of electronic signals by components called CCDs, charge coupled devices. The signals are then recorded as tiny patches of magnetism on to a video tape.

## Display screen
Pictures recorded on the tape can be played back for several viewers on the LCD screen. They can either be saved, or stored for later use to save tape time, or wiped and recorded over if they are not wanted.

## THE SHRINKING CAMCORDER
Early camcorders were so heavy that they had to be held steady with two hands. They were complicated to use and worked only in bright light. Today's versions fit into the palm of the hand. They have simple controls with auto-focus and auto-exposure to adjust the camcorder to suit the changing brightness of the light. They work even in light levels that are almost too dim for the human eye.

# VR HEADSET

## Headset
The computer sends electrical signals to the headset screens which convert these into light rays. The user sees the patterns of rays with his or her eyes and understands them as a scene in his or her brain.

## 3-D vision
In the vision centres at the back of the user's brain, the two slightly different views from the two eyes are merged to give a single view in the 'mind's eye'. This has width, height and also depth or the illusion of distance. It is three-dimensional or 3-D stereoscopic vision.

## Video controls
These knobs control the screen colour, brightness and contrast, as on a normal TV set.

## Speaker
A speaker plays sounds directly into the ear on that side. Some headsets have earpieces or built-in headphones, which help to cut out unwanted sounds from around the user.

## Strap adjuster
The straps are adjusted to suit the head size and shape of the individual user.

## PCB
The main electronic components are fitted into a PCB, printed circuit board. This is made with metal strips already built or 'printed' into it. The components are then fitted on to the board so that the metal strips act as wires to connect them.

## Topstrap
A wide strap passes over the top of the head to join the backstrap at the rear, so that the headset is comfortable.

## Screens
The screens show the images or pictures for the eyes. They show slightly different images for each eye. In real life the two eyes see slightly different views since they look at the scene from slightly different places and directions.

## Audio controls
The audio knobs control the volume of the stereo sound, its balance (whether it is too loud in the left or right ear), and its tone of high and low notes.

## SERIOUS VR

VR systems vary from simple slip-on headsets to full helmets and body suits that look like deep-sea diving suits. These not only provide sight and sound but also physical pressure for the skin's sense of touch and perhaps scents for the nose, too. They also have feedback. They detect the user's movements, so that the computer can alter what he or she sees, hears and feels. The user seems to be moving about in a complete virtual world.

VR can be great fun for flying jet planes, shooting aliens and playing other games. But it also has many serious uses. It helps to train people such as pilots, surgeons, firefighters and rescue workers, where a mistake in the virtual world harms no one.

## TAKING OFF TO NOWHERE

A form of VR has been used for many years in flight simulators where pilots train. The simulator is a whole room and the computer controls large motors or pistons that make it tilt and rock like a real aircraft.

**VR sensory glove**
The glove is an input device. It gathers information, turns it into electrical signals and feeds them into the VR computer for analysis and processing.
In this case the information is about the detailed ways the hand and fingers flex and move to push, pull, grasp, grip and make other actions. Then when the computer shows a hand moving on its screens it can use the data from the glove to make these movements more realistic.

**Sensor wires**
Thin, flexible wires carrying small amounts of electricity are built into the glove. As the wires stretch or bend they alter the amount of electricity passing through them. The computer detects these changes and so can work out how the fingers are moving.

## WHAT IS VIRTUAL REALITY?

It's an object or scene that seems real to the senses of sight, hearing, touch and smell, but is not. It is virtual, or unreal. It exists only as electronic signals in a computer and as spots of light on a screen, sound waves from an earpiece and other ways of stimulating our senses. A central computer processes all the information and sends out the signals to various pieces of equipment. These give us the illusion of seeing, hearing, touching and even smelling, and so we get a sense of reality.

**Finger rings**
The rings gather information about the hand's finger movements and gripping pressure.

# CD PLAYER

### Reflection
A micro-pit on the CD scatters rather than reflects the light that shines up from the laser beam below. The shiny metal between the micro-pits does reflect the beam, which travels back down again.

### Focusing lens
This lens focuses the laser beam to a tiny spot on the disc.

### Reflected laser beam
The reflected laser beam passes down the optical tube towards the light sensors.

### Semi-silvered mirror
The laser beam from the laser is reflected upwards here towards the disc. If the beam is reflected by a shiny flat metal portion between the micro-pits, it passes back down through this mirror to the light sensors below.

### Optical tube
This contains the mirrors, lenses and sensors for the laser beam. It slides along as the screw thread turns to read different parts of the disc.

### Cylindrical lens
A lens makes the reflected laser beam narrower or more focused before it shines on the light sensors.

## STORING INFORMATION

Since its introduction on to the open market in the early 1980s, the CD has proved itself as a small, light, tough, convenient way to store information. An audio CD can store up to 75 minutes of high-quality sound or over 100 million words of text. A CD-ROM (read-only memory) for a computer or similar machine holds about 640 MB (megabytes) of data, programs and other information. Blank CDs are inexpensive and can have the pits 'burned' or 'toasted' into them by a CD burner. They are used for storing computer information.

### Light sensors
A pad of sensors produces a tiny pulse of electricity when illuminated by the reflected laser beam. This is an 'on' or 1 signal of the digital code. A micro-pit on the disc means no reflection, which gives an 'off' or 0 signal.

## Compact disc
The disc is made mainly of plastic and is 12 centimetres (5 inches) across. The working part is its underside, which is coated with a thin layer of shiny aluminium–based metal.

## CD drive motor
Under the CD is a variable speed motor that makes the disc spin around. A vinyl record spins at a constant speed, such as 33.3 turns or revolutions per minute (rpm) for a long player (LP). The CD turns at a varying speed according to whether the inside or outside part of the track is being read, so that the pits and flats always pass the laser beam at a constant rate.

## CD track (underside)
As on a vinyl record, the CD track spirals out from the centre, round and round towards the edge. It is more than 5 kilometres (3 miles) long and contains more than 3 billion micro–pits. The sequence of micro–pits is a code for information.

## Micro–pits (underside)
The micro–pits are microscopic holes or gaps in the CD track. The pits and the flat areas between them are read at the rate of 1.3 million per second.

## Semiconductor laser
A small solid–state laser produces the reddish coloured laser beam for reading the sequences of micro–pits on the disc.

## Ribbon connector
These flexible multi–wire connectors are used to link parts which move in relation to each other, such as the optical tube and the main circuit board in this CD player.

## Optical drive screw
A screw thread turned by an electric motor moves the whole optical tube so that it follows the spiralling track of micro–pits as the disc spins. Unlike a vinyl record, the CD starts playing nearest the middle and finishes out at the edge.

## DIGITAL AND ANALOGUE
The CD is digital. This means it stores information as a sequence or code of numbers or digits. In fact it has only two digits, 0 and 1. The 0 can be thought of as no reflection from the disc where there is a micro-pit. The 1 is a reflection where there isn't a micro-pit. Using two numbers is called binary code. Computers work using binary code, too, making CDs very useful for them.

Analogue systems do not use numbers or on-offs. They use continually varying quantities like a 'wave' of electrical voltage. Although the wave is meant to vary, much smaller natural variations occur within it and mean that it is not an exact way to carry information. As it is played or copied many times, the variations and errors can build up. Copying digital information means copying out lists of 0s and 1s, which is not prone to errors.

# WIDESCREEN TV

### Stereo sound
Two sets of loudspeakers play different sounds for the left and right channels. These reach our left and right ears and give the effect of sounds spread out in front of us across the breadth of the screen. This is known as stereophonic sound.

### Wide sound
Extra loudspeakers positioned to the sides or rear help to spread out the sound. Sometimes a car or plane can be heard approaching from the side before it appears on the screen.

### Subsound
A large loudspeaker built into the TV stand cabinet produces very deep notes. These are not so much heard as felt — for example, the rumble of an earthquake or the boom of a thunderclap.

### Zoom control
The size and proportions of the picture on the screen can be changed with the zoom control.

### Stand
The widescreen TV is very heavy. It has a strong, stable cabinet as a stand. This also stores a VCR and its videotape cassettes, a DVD player and its discs, and perhaps the week's television broadcast guide.

## Pixels

A pixel or picture element is a tiny unit of the screen whose brightness and colour can be controlled. It consists of tiny dots that glow in different colours, red and green and blue. Pixels are built up like spots of colour in a mosaic to make the whole screen picture.

## Picture quality

The quality of a TV picture depends on many features such as the quality of the original electrical signals and the number of lines on the screen. Standard TV screens have pictures made up of some 100,000 pixels arranged in 625 horizontal lines across the screen. The lines are scanned or made to glow from top to bottom.

## TU SCREEN PROPORTIONS

The proportion or ratio of the screen is the length from side to side compared with the height from top to bottom. A typical TV is about 4:3 – that is, one-third again as wide as it is high. However, a full-sized movie screen in a cinema has the ratio 16:9, almost twice as wide as it is high. This was designed to fit comfortably into our field of vision or view, which is the area in front of us that our eyes can see and take in easily. It allows us to watch much broader, more spectacular scenes. Widescreen TV has similar proportions to a movie screen for the same spectacular effect.

## HDTU

Picture quality improves with HD or high definition TV. The screen has more and closer-together horizontal lines, over 1,000, compared to the normal 625.

## Wide screen

The screen is much wider than that of a conventional TV screen. Its proportions suit the natural field of view of our eyes better.

## Words on-screen

Teletext may have over 1,000 pages of writing giving all kinds of information such as news headlines, sports results, weather forecasts and adverts for holidays, money loans and many other items.

## TU SCREEN SIZES

The size of a TV or monitor screen is usually measured diagonally, from one top corner to the bottom opposite corner. However, the edges of the screen may be covered by the frame of the plastic case for the set, so the amount of screen that actually shows the picture is slightly less. A typical smallish 'portable' TV set screen is 35 centimetres (14 inches). A standard domestic TV may be 63 centimetres (25 inches). A widescreen TV may be 100 centimetres (40 inches) or more. The screen is the front of a glass part called a 'tube' (CRT, cathode ray tube or vacuum tube). It looks like a mushroom lying on its side with the 'stalk' projecting backwards. FST is a flatter, squarer tube. The screen surface is flat rather than slightly domed and has more angular rather than rounded corners.

## UCR/DUD

If there are no suitable programmes on terrestrial, satellite or cable TV, the VCR (video cassette recorder-player) and DVD (digital versatile disk player) can show pre-recorded programmes.

# PERSONAL COMPUTER (PC)

### Computer tower
Most of the computer's circuits and drives are housed in a tower unit. This can be placed on a shelf or nearby table if there is not enough room on the desktop.

### Hard disc drive
The hard disc is really a stack of magnetic discs in a case. It is kept in the computer and holds all the computer's programs and data.

### Magnetic disc drive
Removable discs can be placed in this drive. Information is fed from the computer, or written, to the disc and recorded as tiny patches of magnetism on the disc surface. Later the information may be read, or fed back into the computer. This means the discs are read-write rather than read-only.

### Motherboard
The large printed circuit board contains most of the main microchips and components. They include the CPU or central processing unit, which is the computer's 'central brain', and the RAM or random access memory chips, which are its working memory.

### Optical disc drive
Compact discs (CDs) are placed in this drive. They store information as patterns of microscopic pits on their surface and are read optically by laser light. Many computers have read-only optical drives. This means the information stored on them like a memory can only be taken from the disc into the computer. New information cannot be taken from the computer and stored on the disc. So the drive and discs are called CD-ROM, compact disc read-only memory.

### Rear panel
On panels at the back of the computer are sockets and connectors to link it by wires and cables to the monitor screen, keyboard, mouse and extra devices or peripherals.

### Loudspeaker
The computer may be able to play music from its discs or programs. It also makes various beeps, pings and other sounds. These show that it is working properly, has completed a task or is unable to carry out some process.

### Mouse
Moving the mouse moves a pointer or cursor on the screen on to various choices, options, lists and menus. Clicking a button on the mouse selects that choice or option. In image-based programs the mouse can be used like a pen to draw and alter pictures.

### High capacity magnetic drive
Larger magnetic discs that hold more information are slotted in here.

### Mouse mat
This gives a flat but grippy surface for the mouse to roll on. A rubber ball inside the mouse must roll for the mouse to work.

# ADD-ONS

A basic computer usually has a main unit with the circuits and drives, a keyboard, a mouse and a monitor screen. The main unit and screen may be in the same case. But there are dozens of add-ons, plug-ins or peripherals that can be connected to the computer. A common one is the printer to produce 'hard copy' – writing or pictures on paper rather than on the screen. Others that input or send signals to the computer include an image scanner, microphone, digital camera, joystick and music keyboard. Then there are outputs, which receive signals from the computer. These include a hi-fi system, a large and accurate printer called a plotter, image projector and a moving robot arm.

### Monitor screen
The screen works in the same way as the screen of a TV set. But the circuits that receive the signals are not the same. The signals coming from a computer are very different to the signals coming from a TV aerial.

### Screen base
The screen can be swivelled and tilted on its base for the best view and to reduce eyestrain and neckache.

### Alphanumeric keys
The letters of the alphabet from A–Z and the standard numerals from 0 –9 are on this area of the keyboard, laid out in the same way as on the traditional typewriter.

### Special function keys
Usually labelled F1, F2 and so on, these are 'short-cut' keys that have special jobs according to the program being used. For example, one of them may bring up a particular list or menu of choices.

### Numeric function keys
As well as being used simply for numbers, these keys can be given special jobs, such as moving the cursor or pointer up one paragraph in a written document.

# COMPUTER TERMINALS

The computer shown here is a complete working unit and can be used on its own. A computer terminal may look similar. But it is usually just a screen, keyboard and mouse. These are connected by longer wires or a network to a main computer. Many other terminals are connected too. Lots of people can use the same computer at the same time, sharing the information and programs.

# VIDEOPHONE

**LCD**
The small screen does not use a 'tube' like a normal television set. It has a much flatter, lighter liquid crystal display (LCD).

**Flip-up screen**
The screen is lit and activated by tilting or lifting it up at an angle. This also switches on the videophone's camera.

**Earpiece**
This works in the opposite way to the mouthpiece. It receives electrical signals along its wire and converts them into sound waves that you can hear.

**Loudspeaker**
The loudspeaker produces the sound of the other person's voice if the handset is not being used. It has to give out only a limited range of sound pitches or frequencies, those produced by the voice, compared to the music of a full orchestra. So it can be small and simple compared to a proper music system loudspeaker.

**Digital display**
Telephone numbers and other information are displayed here.

**Telephone handset**
This works in the same way as the normal telephone handset, so you can speak to and hear the person at the other end of the line.

**Mouthpiece**
The mouthpiece is a simple microphone that picks up the sound waves from your voice and converts them into patterns of electrical signals. This is the opposite of the earpiece. The signals go along wires in the curly cord into the videophone.

## LCD TECHNOLOGY

A liquid crystal display (LCD) is much smaller, flatter and lighter than the 'tube' for a normal television screen. However, its picture isn't quite as sharp and clear. In an LCD tiny spots of coloured crystalline substances, like coloured jelly, let through or stop light by a certain amount according to how much electricity is passed through them. In the backlit display the light comes from the lowest or base layer of screen behind the crystals, passes through them and shines into the eyes. This is brighter than the non-backlit version, where light from the surroundings is reflected off the back of the screen. Most digital watches have non-backlit LCD displays. Backlit are used in laptop and palmtop computers, in miniature and wristwatch TVs, and in some giant screens at sports stadia, music concerts and similar big events.

## Camera
The camera uses CCD technology to take several photographs of your face every second as you sit in front of the videophone. These are converted into patterns of electrical signals and sent along the phone line with the voice signals, to be displayed on the screen at the other end.

## Screen controls
These small knobs adjust the screen's brightness, colours and contrast as for a normal television.

## Numerical pad
You press the buttons to call another telephone number in the usual way. You also use the numbers in combination with other buttons to programme various functions into the machine.

## Function buttons
The videophone can be programmed in various ways using these buttons, such as to recall a phone number at a certain time or call it every so many minutes.

## Circuits
Most of the electronic components are fixed to a single PCB – printed circuit board – inside the videophone.

## Mains or battery
Ordinary voice-only phones are powered by the electrical signals coming along the telephone wire. The videophone needs extra electricity for its screen so it has the option of batteries or plug-in mains power.

## A JUMPY PICTURE
When a full colour picture is converted into electrical signals, even at the small size of the videophone screen shown here, the result is many thousands of signals. If the picture is designed to show movement, this becomes millions of signals per second. Most phone lines are unable to carry this much information. They are designed for the relatively limited number of signals representing the sound of the voice. Because of this limited capacity, only a small colour picture can be sent and this can change only a few times a second, producing a jumping or flickering image.

# MEDICAL SCANNER

## Rotating drum
The drum inside the casing twists so that the magnets and detectors can rotate around the body and scan it from different angles.

## Superconducting magnets
Very powerful magnets 'magnetize' the body for a short period and affect the way the billions of hydrogen atoms in its parts and tissues line up and spin around. (Hydrogen, H, is one of the most common chemical elements in the body, making up part of each water molecule, $H_2O$ – and the body is almost two-thirds water.)

## Patient
The patient lies still on a bed-like table. He or she may be given a sedative to relax the body and mind and ease any worries. A particular substance or chemical may also be injected into the patient to make certain kinds of scan clearer.

## Scanner casing
The working parts of the scanner are contained inside a strong metal case, to protect the people on the outside and the delicate circuits and components inside.

## Sliding table
The table slides to move the patient along so that successive horizontal levels or sections of the body can be scanned, one at a time. This builds up a 3-D image.

## Connecting cables
Thick cables containing many individual wires link the scanner and control console.

## Radio units
Radio waves are beamed through the magnetized body and affect the way the hydrogen atoms line up and spin. As they alter their alignment and spin, the atoms send out their own tiny pulses of radio waves, which are detected by the radio sensors. They form electrical signals, which are sent to the computer along with signals about the angle, strength and timing of the beams.

## A WORRYING EXPERIENCE
Having a scan can be a worrying process. But it is painless and usually over very quickly. Modern scanning machines are as harmless as they can be made, and there are virtually no risks.

**Viewing window**
Operators can watch through the window to check all is well with the patient and equipment. The glass is specially strengthened and treated for protection.

**Monitor screen**
The scan images are shown on the TV-style computer monitor screens. Different body parts such as nerves, bones and blood have different amounts of brightness or intensity. These can be colour-coded by the computer to make the differences clearer.

**Protective screen**
A protective wall surrounds the operators and other people and shields them from any harmful effects of the scanning equipment. For an individual patient who is in the room for a short time the risks are almost zero. But they increase for the operators and other staff who are there hour after hour, week after week.

**Computer**
Huge amounts of computer power are needed to decode the signals coming in from the radio sensors and other equipment, analyse them and gradually build up the scan pictures section by section.

**Controls**
The operator controls the computer, which controls the scanner and other equipment. Most of the instructions are fed in by typing on to the keyboard as with a normal computer.

**Operator**
The operator is highly skilled in various areas including medicine, human anatomy (body structure), computer operations and engineering.

## TYPES OF MEDICAL IMAGING

There are many ways of looking inside the body without cutting it open:

• X-rays are useful for showing bones and teeth. Modern X-rays are very safe but strong X-rays can harm the body.

• CT (computerized tomography or CAT, computerized axial tomography) uses weak X-rays that are not harmful. It scans the body slice by slice and puts the slices together for a detailed 3-D result.

• An ultrasound scan beams sound waves, too high-pitched for our hearing, into the body and analyses the echoes. It is used to examine babies in the womb.

• The MR (magnetic resonance imaging) scan gets detailed results by putting the body in a powerful magnetic field and beaming radio waves through it.

• PET (positron emission tomography) involves injecting 'tagged' substances into the body, such as hormones or blood sugar. The scanner tracks the substance and shows how it is used. PET scans are often used on the brain.

# INTERNET

## LOGGING ON TO THE NET

The Internet is the worldwide international network of interlinked computers and other electronic devices. It is not really one single network but complex groups of smaller networks joined together. You need a computer that plugs into the phone line or telecom system to use it. You 'log on' by sending signals to your ISP, Internet service provider. The ISP's own computer acts as a go-between or intermediate between your computer and the whole network. You 'download' by receiving along the phone line the electrical signals that represent various forms of information such as words, pictures, sounds and computer programs, and storing these in your computer.

### Global telecom network
The telecommunications network involves telephone exchanges, computers of all shapes and sizes, fax machines, landlines, microwave and satellite links and many other parts.

### E-mail
'E' or electronic mail does not use paper. You type or make a message on your computer, address it to the recipient and send it along the telephone line to your e-mail provider. The message waits there, stored on what is effectively a huge computer disc, until the recipient uses his or her computer to call up and collect it.

### Modem link
The modem is a device that changes the tiny digital electronic pulses inside the computer into electrical signals suitable for feeding into the telecom network.

### Back/Forwards
Clicking on these arrows goes to the previous page you were looking at on the screen, or to the next page on the list.

### Address
The address is not a physical place like a house or office. It is an electronic label for a certain website or e-mail recipient – more like the address of their computer.

### Option panels or buttons
You can choose what to see next by using the mouse to position the computer's cursor or arrow on one of these panels or 'screen buttons' and then clicking the mouse.

### Mouse

## THE WEB

Imagine a vast library of books, pictures, movies, adverts, music, catalogues and other works and publications. The World Wide Web is like this but in electronic form. It exists as tiny electrical signals inside computers and whizzing along telephone lines. You can look up a website, which is like taking a library book or catalogue off the shelf. This is usually made by one company or organization and it is about a certain subject. You can look at the different pages on screen just as you would flick through the book. But using the Web is far quicker than visiting a library. Web sites can be continents away. They can be changed and updated at any time. Unlike a book, they are two-way – you can send information, messages, orders and money to them as well as receiving goods or information from them.

### Destination computer
The message from your computer can reach another computer on the opposite side of the world in just one second. However, the various delays and changes as it passes through the system mean that the transfer time is usually slightly longer.

### Search engine
You can search the Net using a search engine. This is a computer program or application that scans the network for the key words or phrases that you enter, and shows you a list of possible addresses that might be helpful. You can search in a certain country, a continent or across the whole world.

### Hub
A hub is a concentrated centre where many big computers send and receive information rapidly. Gateway computers change information or data into the different forms and codes, called protocols, used in various countries.

### ISP or Server

### Screen and page
A page may be more than just what you can see on your screen. You may have to move or scroll the page sideways or down so you can see the rest of it as it comes on to the screen. It's like moving the large page of a newspaper or magazine around behind a smaller opening, which is the screen.

### Image
Pictures tend to download (arrive in your computer) more slowly than words. They can be copied into the memory of your own computer, but they take up much more memory space than words.

### Text
Words usually download, or come into your computer, very quickly. You can highlight or choose them, copy them into your own computer's memory, then store them in one of your own files or documents.

### User's computer

# SATELLITE NAVIGATION SYSTEM

### Comsat
A communications satellite is part of the worldwide telecom network. It receives and sends on radio signals for telephone calls, TV programmes, computer messages and many other forms of long-distance communication.

### Dish antenna
The large dish can send and receive faint or faraway signals. It can be moved by electric motors and pointed very precisely at a certain satellite, and moved to link with other satellites at different times.

### Ground station
This is in communication with many satellites via its large dish and other aerials. It also contacts other stations on the ground by terrestrial radio and microwave links, and by the cables and landlines of the telecom network.

### Ship to shore
Direct radio links between a ship and land can only be carried out over limited distances. Too far away and the curve of the Earth's surface gets in the way, since most radio signals go in straight lines and not around bends. This is why satellites are so useful. They can receive signals on the uplink and then beam them down somewhere else a continent away. They act like relay or passing-on radio sets on incredibly tall towers.

### Satellite orbit
A satellite has forward motion, which means that it tries to go in a straight line. It would fly off into space, but the Earth's gravity pulls it down. However, the satellite is pulled down at a rate that matches the way the Earth's surface curves around beneath. So the satellite endlessly falls to Earth, but never gets there, because the Earth endlessly curves away from it. Round and round and ...

# THE SPEED OF LIGHT

Radio and microwave signals go up and down to satellites at the fastest possible speed, the speed of light. This is about 300,000 kilometres per second (186,000 miles per second). However, some satellites are so far away that signals take more than one-tenth of a second to get there. If the signals go up and down to several satellites on their journey around the globe, the delay can add up to almost a second!

# GSO

Most satellites seem to move across the sky when seen from down here on Earth. But a satellite 35,787 kilometres (about 22,000 miles) directly above the Equator has an orbit speed that means it goes once around the Earth in 24 hours. The Earth itself spins around once in the same time. So looking up from the surface of Earth, the satellite seems to hover or hang in the same place all the time. This orbit is called a geostationary or geosynchronous orbit, GSO. It means that dish aerials do not have to move or tilt to track the satellite across the sky. They can be left pointing in one direction at it. GSO is used for several types of satellite, especially those which broadcast satellite TV programmes into our homes.

## SARSAT

Many ships, planes and vehicles carry a SARSAT radio beacon or transmitter. In case of trouble or emergency this sends out radio signals on an emergency channel. The signals are picked up by a world system of SARSATs, Search And Rescue SATellites. The SARSATs send alert signals down to ground stations. The time delay for the radio signals from the emergency transmitter reaching the various SARSATs in their different positions gives the location of the transmitter, and so the search and rescue can begin.

## Navigation beacon

A lighthouse sends out pulses of light. The length and pattern of the pulses is a code for the identity of the lighthouse. In the same way a radio beacon sends out radio signals for its own identity or 'name', showing ships that it is nearby. The time delay between the radio signals from several beacons allows you to work out your own position in relation to them.

# Index